AWESOME ATHLETES

TROY AIKMAN

Paul Joseph
ABDO & Daughters

Published by Abdo & Daughters, 4940 Viking Drive, Suite 622, Edina, Minnesota 55435.

Copyright © 1997 by Abdo Consulting Group, Inc., Pentagon Tower, P.O. Box 36036, Minneapolis, Minnesota 55435 USA. International copyrights reserved in all countries. No part of this book may be reproduced in any form without written permission from the publisher.

Printed in the United States.

Cover and Interior Photo credits: Wide World Photos
                                  Allsport USA

Edited by Kal Gronvall

Library of Congress Cataloging-in-Publication Data

Joseph, Paul, 1970-
Troy Aikman / Paul Joseph.
        p.   cm. — (Awesome athletes)
Includes index.
Summary: A brief biography covering the personal life and football career of the Dallas Cowboys quarterback who was named Most Valuable Player in the 1992 season's Super Bowl.
ISBN 1-56239-643-9
1. Aikman, Troy, 1966-   --Juvenile literature. 2. Football players—United States—Biography—Juvenile literature. 3. Dallas Cowboys (Football team)—Juvenile literature. [l. Aikman, Troy, 1966- . 2. Football players.] I. Title. II. Series.
GV939.A46J67 1997
796.332'092—dc20
[B]`   96-16088
                                                                 CIP
                                                                 AC

Contents

Slingin' Cowboy

In 1989, many new changes occurred for the Dallas Cowboys. One of them was that a new owner took over. Jerry Jones bought the Cowboys for $140 million dollars. Then he fired legendary coach, Tom Landry, who had been with Dallas since its first season in 1960. Jones hired an old friend, Jimmy Johnson, to coach the Cowboys.

Two weeks later Johnson attended the **National Football League (NFL) draft**. Johnson made one of the best decisions of his career. He used his very first pick in the 1989 draft on quarterback Troy Aikman.

The team and fans were excited about Troy becoming their new quarterback. Jerry Rhome, the Cowboys' quarterback coach, described Troy this way: "If you sat down to build an NFL quarterback, Troy is what you'd come up with. He's 6 feet, 4 inches, 222 pounds, great arm strength—everything's perfect."

It didn't take long for Troy to lead the Cowboys to greatness. Football fans everywhere could see that Troy would soon become one of the greatest quarterbacks in **NFL** history.

In just three years Troy led the Cowboys from being the worst team in the league—with a 1-15 **record**—to making the **playoffs**.

Behind the strength of Troy's arm and leadership, and the great running of Emmitt Smith, the Cowboys dominated the league the next four years. From 1992 to 1995, the Cowboys won an incredible three **Super Bowls**.

Without that first **draft** pick in 1989, the Cowboys wouldn't have Troy, and it is likely they wouldn't have three more Super Bowl titles. But success didn't come easily for Troy, as he had to overcome many **obstacles** to reach the top. But he worked hard and was determined to be a great NFL quarterback.

Young Cowboy

Troy Kenneth Aikman was born November 21, 1966, in Cerritos, California, just outside of Los Angeles. His father, Kenneth, was a welder, then became a **farmer**. His mother, Charlyn, was a **homemaker**.

Troy was born with crooked feet. To correct the problem, he wore casts up to his knees. When he learned to walk, the casts were replaced with special shoes. At night his mother would strap the heels of his shoes together to help his feet grow straight.

Once Troy's feet were corrected, he began playing sports. Football was his favorite.

When Troy was 12 years old, his father took a new job in **rural** Oklahoma. The Aikmans moved into a house on a 172-acre **ranch** outside of the small town of Henryetta, about 100 miles north of Dallas. There they raised cattle, pigs, and chickens.

At first, Troy missed California and thought Oklahoma was boring. He had grown up in a big city and now the family didn't even have neighbors. But after a while he began to like the quiet life and small-town atmosphere in Oklahoma.

Oklahoma Sooners' quarterback Troy Aikman is pursued by Miami defenseman Bruce Fleming.

Three-Sport Star

Troy became very popular at his high school because of his great athletic ability. He excelled in three sports: baseball, basketball, and, of course, football—lettering in all three.

Many colleges were interested in him for all three sports. He easily could have received a baseball **scholarship** to a big-time college as a pitcher. But Troy never even considered this. He chose to focus on a college football career so he could reach his goal to someday play for his favorite team, the Dallas Cowboys.

As a quarterback for Henryetta High, Troy was incredible. People couldn't believe the talent that he had. Although college **scouts** wanted him because of his great athletic skill, his team didn't win many games.

Still everyone knew that Troy was going to go places. After one high school game, the coach from the opposing team was so impressed with Troy that he came up to him and said, "We'll be watching you someday on *Monday Night Football.*"

Although Troy had a lot of natural talent, his best attribute was his work ethic. Troy was always the first one on the practice field and the last one to leave. Sometimes he would stay out an extra hour or two to work on sprints and throw the ball in the 100-degree heat!

UCLA's Troy Aikman passes the football during team practice.

Choosing A College

When Troy was a sophomore in high school, colleges were already trying to **recruit** him. The football coach from Oklahoma State University, a man named Jimmy Johnson, really wanted Troy to play for him. But Troy decided to accept a **scholarship** to the University of Oklahoma, which had one of the best football teams in the nation.

The head coach of Oklahoma, Barry Switzer, who would later coach Troy in the **NFL**, used primarily a **running offense**. But he told Troy that he would change it to a **passing offense** if Troy would come to Oklahoma.

But things didn't change when Troy came. By the time the season started, Oklahoma was still in a running offense, and Troy ended up watching from the bench most of his freshman season. Troy was the starting quarterback his sophomore year but the running offense was still in place. Troy was beginning to have second thoughts about staying with the team.

Then something bad happened. In the fourth game of the season Troy dropped back to pass and was sacked by two players. He grabbed his left leg in pain. His leg was broken.

While his leg healed, Troy thought about his football career. He wondered if he should quit football, but that thought quickly left his mind. He thought about switching schools. He wasn't playing well at Oklahoma, and he hated the running offense. He wanted to play where he could throw the ball. Troy decided to transfer to another school.

Back to California

Again Jimmy Johnson tried to **recruit** Troy. Johnson was now the head coach at the University of Miami. Johnson's offense was suited perfectly for Troy. It was a pro-style offense, which meant that there was a lot of passing. Troy thought he would be happy playing football for Miami.

But it wasn't to be. Although Troy liked Johnson and the offense, he didn't like the city or the school. So he decided against Miami and went back to Los Angeles.

Troy decided to attend the University of California at Los Angeles (UCLA). And the choice couldn't have been better for him.

Troy loved UCLA's **passing offense**, and he had two very productive seasons. He set school **records** for most touchdown passes in a season, most completed passes in a season, and most completed passes in a single game.

In only two seasons he came close to breaking passing **records** set by quarterbacks who had played for four years. UCLA was 20-4 in two seasons with Troy at quarterback. And in those seasons the team also won two bowl games.

After his final season, Troy received the Davey O'Brien National Quarterback Award, given to the best college quarterback in the country. And he was named College Quarterback of the Year by the Quarterback Club. Troy also finished third in the voting for the Heisman Trophy, given to the best college player in any position.

UCLA's Troy Aikman (8) shakes loose from Washington's defenseman Dennis Brown (79).

Jimmy Finally Gets His Man

In 1989, the Cowboys had a new owner, a new coach, and they were about to get a new quarterback. Jimmy Johnson was the new Dallas coach, and he was not going to let Troy Aikman get away from him for the third time.

Johnson used his number one pick in the **draft** to get his quarterback. And the feeling was mutual. Troy wanted to be a Cowboy just as much as Jimmy wanted him to be. It was a dream come true for Troy, who was now playing for his favorite football team.

The Cowboys gave Troy the highest **rookie contract** ever signed. Jones and Johnson wanted Troy happy and everyone knew that he was the future of the Cowboys.

But Troy's first season with the Cowboys was no fun at all. He took so many hard hits and was getting sacked so often that he thought he wouldn't be able to finish out his **contract**. He broke a finger, had a concussion, and was sore all over after every game. Even worse, the team finished 1-15.

The only bright spot that year was the game against the Phoenix Cardinals. Troy passed for 379 yards, setting a new **NFL record** for most passing yards completed by a **rookie**.

Everyone knew after that game Troy had what it takes to be a great quarterback and lead his team to the **Super Bowl**. But they also knew that he couldn't do it alone. Troy needed a supporting cast.

Dallas Cowboys head coach, Jimmy Johnson, hugs Troy Aikman.

Troy Aikman during his days at UCLA.

1966	1978	1984	1987
Born November 21 in Cerritos, California.	Moves to Oklahoma.	Accepts scholarship to Oklahoma University.	Transfers to UCLA; leads team to Aloha Bowl victory.

How Awesome Is He?

Aikman's MVP performance in Super Bowl XXVII compares favorably with other MVPs of the big game.

PLAYER	YEAR	COMP.	YARDS	TDs	RATING
Phil Simms	1987	22	268	3	150.9
Joe Montana	1990	22	297	5	147.6
Jim Plunkett	1981	13	261	3	145.1
Troy Aikman	**1993**	**22**	**273**	**4**	**140.7**
Doug Williams	1988	18	340	4	128.1

TROY AIKMAN

TEAM: DALLAS COWBOYS
NUMBER: 8
POSITION: QUARTERBACK
HEIGHT: 6 FEET 4 INCHES
WEIGHT: 225 LBS.

1989	1991	1993	1994	1996
Drafted by the Dallas Cowboys.	Leads Cowboys to their first winning season since 1985.	Throws 4 TDs in Super Bowl; named Super Bowl MVP.	Leads the Cowboys to their second-consecutive Super Bowl win.	Leads the Cowboys to victory in Super Bowl XXX.

- 🏈 **1987 Pac 10 Offensive Player of the Year**
- 🏈 **3-Time Super Bowl Champ**
- 🏈 **1993 NFL Completion Percentage Leader**
- 🏈 **1993 Super Bowl MVP**
- 🏈 **5-Time Pro Bowl Selection**

Highlights

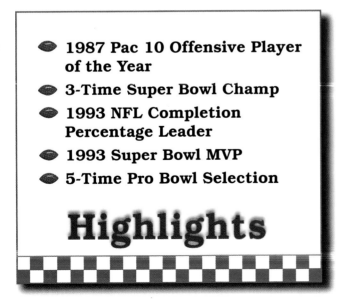

That Helps

In 1990, the Cowboys **drafted** running back Emmitt Smith. Smith was the kind of runner who was an all-around threat. Teams had to concentrate on him, so that gave Troy more time to throw. The Cowboys also added some big offensive **linemen** to block for Troy, and the defense was also improving.

The Cowboys were starting to play like a team, and things were looking up for them. They finished the season with a 7-9 **record**.

The 1991 season was a breakthrough for both Troy and the Cowboys. They were starting to show their **Super Bowl** form. Troy finished the season with the most passing yards and the highest completion rate of any quarterback in the National Football Conference (NFC). He was chosen to be in the **Pro Bowl**—football's All-Star game.

The Cowboys earned a spot in the **playoffs** with an 11-5 regular season **record**. After a first-round victory over the Chicago Bears they were beaten by the Detroit Lions. But the Cowboys were on the upswing.

Quarterback Troy Aikman releases a pass against the San Diego Chargers.

The Dream Season

The 1992 season was a dream come true for Troy. The Cowboys began the season by beating the defending **Super Bowl** champions, the Washington Redskins, on national television. They ended the year winning the Super Bowl.

The Cowboys raced through the regular season with a 13-3 **record**, behind Troy's unheard of numbers, including his completing an amazing 85 percent of his passes in one game. Then came the **playoffs** where they beat the Philadelphia Eagles, 34-10.

In the NFC championship game, Troy worked his magic again. After a 10-10 tie going into halftime, Troy came out in the second half and completed 13 of 16 passes. The final score was Dallas 30, San Francisco 20.

Troy completed a playoff record of 70 percent of his passes and had thrown for 322 yards! In just four years, Troy had led his team to the Super Bowl.

In the **Super Bowl**, Troy and the Cowboys dominated, crushing the Buffalo Bills, 52-17. For his efforts, Troy was named the Super Bowl **Most Valuable Player (MVP)**. It was a great way to end the dream season.

Under pressure Aikman lets go a pass against the Bills during Super Bowl XXVII.

Back-to-Back

Not much changed in 1993. Troy was still one of the best quarterbacks in the league, and the Cowboys were in the **Super Bowl** for the second-straight year.

After walking through the **playoffs**, they met up with the Buffalo Bills again. And again Dallas dominated the game, winning 30-13 behind Troy's passing and Emmitt's running.

In five years, Troy had two Super Bowls, and was showing the world that he was the best quarterback in the league.

Opposite page: Troy Aikman passing against the Bills in the Super Bowl.

Not Him Again

In 1994, after a **conflict** between owner Jerry Jones and coach Jimmy Johnson, Johnson was let go. Jones hired Troy's former college coach Barry Switzer. Troy really liked Johnson, but didn't care very much for Switzer, especially after the treatment he had received from Switzer in college. But Troy stayed a professional and played very well.

Troy had another fine year, earning a selection to his fourth-straight **Pro Bowl**. The Cowboys also did well, going all the way to the NFC Championship game before losing to San Francisco. They were only one game from their third-straight **Super Bowl**.

Troy Aikman with his new head coach, Barry Switzer.

Back Again

It didn't take very long to get back to the **Super Bowl**. In 1995, after one year of not being in the Super Bowl, Troy led the Cowboys to their third **NFL** title in four years.

After a great regular season, they walked through the **playoffs**, beating the Green Bay Packers in the NFC championship game.

In the Super Bowl, the Cowboys held on in a hard-fought game against the Pittsburgh Steelers. Again, Troy and the Cowboys were Super Bowl Champions.

Opposite page: In Super Bowl XXX Troy Aikman led the Cowboys to a 27-17 victory over the Pittsburgh Steelers.

What's Next?

Troy has accomplished everything a quarterback can accomplish. Through hard work—and struggling through the difficult times—he has shown everyone how to accomplish their goals.

Although Troy wants to continue playing football and winning more championships for the Cowboys, he does enjoy other activities. He sings in a country band with other Dallas football players. They call themselves the Super Boys. He also likes donating his time and money by working for special **charities** such as the American Cancer Society, Easter Seals, Special Olympics, and the United Way.

Even more, Troy has set up **scholarships** at his former high school and college. He also donated $20,000 to build a health and fitness center for young people in Henryetta.

Troy sometimes feels the pressure of being the best in the league, but he knows he wants to stay on top. And judging from his past, it is easy to see that he always will be.

Cowboy quarterback Troy Aikman.

GLOSSARY

athlete - Someone who is physically skilled and talented at sports.

charities - A fund or organization for helping the poor, the sick, and the helpless.

conflict - A difference in opinion that ends in an argument and is hard to resolve.

contract - A legal document signed by players that states how much money they will get paid and how many years they will play for a particular team.

draft - An event held in April where NFL teams choose college players. The team with the worst record the previous year gets the first pick.

farmer - A person who raises crops or animals on a farm.

homemaker - A person who works at home, taking care of household needs and raising children.

linemen - Players in football who block for the quarterback and running backs.

Most Valuable Player (MVP) - An award given to the best player in the league or in the Super Bowl.

National Football League (NFL) - A professional football league in the United States consisting of a National and American Conference, each with 15 teams.

obstacle - Something that stands in the way of accomplishing something.

passing offense - A type of offense in football where they pass the ball most of the time.

playoffs - Games played by the best teams after the regular season is over to determine a champion.

Pro Bowl - An all-star game played at the end of the season in Hawaii. The best players at their positions get to play.

ranch - A very large farm and the buildings on it, where people raise animals.

record - The best it has ever been done in a certain event.

recruit - Trying to get people to go to your school because they have a certain talent.

rookie - A first-year player in the NFL.

running offense - A type of offense in football where they run the ball most of the time.

rural - An area outside the city limits in the country.

scholarship - A money award used to pay for school given to someone for their particular skills.

scouts - The people who watch athletes play football and determine if they have what it takes to make it at a higher level.

signing bonus - Extra money paid to players after they sign their contract.

Super Bowl - The NFL championship game, played between the American and National conference champions.

Index